# Words are weapons

## Jessica Mourning

BookLeaf Publishing

India | USA | UK

Presentation by *BookLeaf Publishing*

Web: www.bookleafpub.com

E-mail: info@bookleafpub.com

ISBN: 9789357214889

First edition 2022

# ACKNOWLEDGEMENT

Forever indebted to my healing. This is a cleansing of my palate, a softened sanctuary for my dictation.

# PREFACE

These pages are parts of everything within me. I, personified. You never really know a person until you read their thoughts, well...here some are mine.

# Blisters

I'm small on concrete
I'm small on grass
I'm small on a blue rock
Secular universe
you plant me,
to breathe me
Flow of the well
I'm well to do.
I'm still dormant in shoes
the blisters on my heals remind me
I'm a walking stick
with a sorted purpose.
What that is I'm provided the answers in
bruised breaths
burnt lungs
not crispy
Spring renews
blossomed sacked breaths
how I hold you behind closed lips
When I scream from within
I haven't screamed out yet,
When I do, I'm afraid
I'll quake the earth
just a tremble
A small thimble

can sow the damage you reaped
an effervescent peepshow
Red light shine
my shadow
This muse, a canvas
you shit on.
I look out the window and see
the yellow ball
bounce up and down in a day
I see the shadows you
throw at play.
Thankfully, no more
and never again.
I walk
still blistered, but I'll heal up.

# Battles

Vehemently, I forge through with intense
recognition
only from myself.
No one else sees my battles alas
I will have to fight them alone.
Why so many battles, I'm exhausted.
by battles I mean everything from alarms going
off to the sun going down
All this warfare and I am without shield on
opposing days
Oh, I fight, I will till' the death
When I say without shield, it's all I wasn't
prepared for...
I like preparation, my ocd, neurosis, and
beautiful anxiety
runs the gambit...


my likely scheduled forgetfulness is a mixed
breed delightfulness
I implore I'll always be this way,
As I age, I'm just learning to let it brand me
instead of it being invisible ink
Only noticeable when I decide it to be.
Or that's what I've fixed myself into believing.

Invisible ink girl, was the let's do whatever you
want girl
laughable good time: drink a beer, pop a pill, the
suns up girl.
The end girl.
I have branded myself with no more, I am
altered with detailed trauma
definition I prefer is developing...myself, slowly.
Try to understand, I'm nomadic by choice...and I
am fond of its peace.
In small increments, when this secular space, my
universe allows me with such tranquility
I soak it up, it's in no way an immortal sequence
There is always a battle cry
such screeching allotments of time
I allow constant absorption of myself; I need
good measure to breathe.
I am who I wanted to be years ago...clean and
learning my purpose
That is my immortality figuring, it figures it
would be.
Learning to change is the optimal echo of
oneself
My patterns, shifting/sifting through what is left,
or has been found within.
My shield is transparency, and not many want
the same type of candor
Who wants to be a burden.

# Arsonist

Does anyone really love fully
or do we box ourselves into our own pixelated
wants
of when the times right
we fit ourselves in anothers time, so ours seem
not so lonely
we bore into straightlined feelings, boxed shaped
houses
another god damn dream
a waste of time, I say
we make another our home until the whole shit
box goes up in flames
with our precious minutes, hours...ourselves
trauma is flammable...and who isn't doused in
kerosene
Love, thought of love the want is a terrible idea
I'll straddle the fence of love...for longing of
tettering
I seem to only get invitations from pyros.
when it seems I am the true arsonist.

# Saddist

What do you think I am
a saddist
a broken clown
Here lies the cheap trick
the girl I used to be
every care in the world
with broken shoulders
I carry wounds that you couldnt fathom
but with emptied mouth
you'll hear
you'll hear it all
I clawed my way outta hell
through the limbo passage
in which I still reside
You'll all be here
some are and just dont know it
You'll feel the scratching
clevered nailed karma
You doubt it
maybe you just have limited perspective
maybe you aren't ready
Maybe you aren't ready for me.

# My mothers window

My mother's window
is as square as I am
open it up and you shall find opportunity
I am so
unequal to the other sides
Im the broken length
its needed but squeaks
its just a window
I see my broken self through
a paneled reflection that I'm framed into
Im two dots flat in dimenson
I'm stuck in the lamence of this
the true reflection of this is no one will
understand.
there are four sides to her window
and I'm the broken one.

# Yellow

Yellow, I say sunburst.
truly unique in madness
prose with a rose
its my dime, I ryhme.
You really have no idea where I am,
anymore
I'm a time left ticking
I barely remember but the clock kept good
magnatism.
I was never a wind up
I spun my own spindle
A difference in how I feel, just a course...of
discourse.
just gradual rotation of kindled memories.
some succulent, some uneasy.
I always like the uneasy
I'm a difficult rhythm to hum, you'll whistle my
name,
you will.

# Red flag

You see faces in the shower
I feel hands I dont remember
sychronicity
How many senses have we burned
or red flagged on each other
You were the only part of me that made sense
a warmth that caught me a blaze
I still have burns, aches and pains
My spine has born a piece of you
He is alone
You are the one to leave
and yes, I am in the fire alone...that you helped
kindle.
unfair corespondence at its best
one visit and a phone call through me.
Anger is a temple I set afire to show you where
home is
go ahead and purse your lips to the lies to keep
you at bay
Thats how you justify it
you are just.

# Unkind bitch

going to begin
to try to change
my existence
Haven't we all said or thought that?
Nerves get in the way of everything
always have
Trauma is a tricky, unkind bitch
I guess depending on the magnitude of our
traumas therein lies our existence
I wish I could wake up one day and not go over
every scenario
The experiences, life I've missed out on.
The hardest part is people just see you as lazy,
unmotivated
They only see externally
if only people felt a person instead of seeing
My dad never wants to hear anything,
never has.
I know we all have one person we wish could
hear us
not just wanting to only hear the positive
like they wear pessimistic earmuffs
Selective emotional hearing
It's hard to never be heard, like really heard
I know trauma makes you isolate

that's where I am
I've hermited myself in platos cave
all I see are Shadows of people I used to know
You go through the years thinking people
genuinely know you
I guess it depends on what type of people you've
surrounded yourself with,
to only find they don't know you at all.
I know there are others like myself, disassociate.

# Galoshes

I've noticed I write from an "I'm" perspective
Nothin good comes from that place
I am
I am
breaking the contraction
putting myself back together
contradicting myself
with brute punctuation
language is fluid
yet I drown in it anymore
Not the way you'd think,
like an overflowing river
a constant feeling
I am separate
Stagnant puddle jumper
with no galoshes.

# A part of me

I am on an island
Pearled skin from the sand crests of time.
The tides break the solitudal echoes of
aloneness.
Fresh air, salt licked tongue.
The rain cleanses and keeps me afloat.
Survival, foregoing.
I feast on others regret daily.
I sink down and realize I am alone.
Sequestered, but ideally content.
My, is no longer mine.
I have nothing
I am bare and burned.
Apollo ever overshadowing
I stay out of the false light.
I stay in the shade & relax by twilight.
My relief is my knowledge of my truths,
I carry their burdens effortlessly to the fire
idiocy entrails smoke risen passages:
tomorrow all over again, the same as before
nothing changes only if I leave my unsafe safety,
then I'll explore.
This island is indifferent from the grounds where
I used to sink my feet
its corse and on fire,

it tears me apart from my soft skin.
I am alone,
no ships break the blue line of forever
no rescue yet.
I stay in loving silence,
when able to be with my own thoughts.
Will I last, undecidedly so
only the waves, sand, and trees will know.
Optimist outlook,
I awake with the salted sleep of dreams,
of comforted home.
Still here, but grateful to hear the birds at play
a symphony of my life I cry for each day.
Stranded isn't just a state of mind
when every resource keeps you in a continual
stride of backstrokes,
it's a ritual just to keep me swimming.
I love the water but too much of the salty sea is
draining
coals still left from the fire before boil down to
quench my thirst.
My body is depleting but I still smile when I
wake
I love the swim,
I pray for an open break.
Wave me in and save me out,
I'm stronger on sand than I'd once realized
My health is the only burden of heart,
in which I sympathize.

Look out and mirage yourself with saviour.
I dreamed I floated away in safeties fleet,
no more adversaries I will meet.
Stepping lightly in patterned steps softened the
burns at times,
the salted water sooted the stagnancy of pain.
A part of me, I left there.
The weakened state I was surviving in was
saved.
A rescue away from where it was,
to know where I'm safely going.
My soul eclipsed, renewed and stolen away from
that island where I laid,
never completely losing breath.
Still fortunate enough, hopefully, I escape only
slightly concaved.
Kindled pieces of my boat break on shore,
as I stare back at that experience,
only to leave, with joy.

.

# Trivial pursuit

I fall back
Reglimpse the traces,
the places I've been
Outlined focus-foolish dreams.
I've been lied to.
My life shaken,
a trivial pursuit that's not my own.
To feel owned and put on a shelf,
a grief I awaken to everyday.
I miss breathing
truly a full exhale of sweet relief.
A deserved bereavement to solidify to the heart,
for wasted time.
I'm trying to salvage the moments I remember
dearly.

# I used to

I used to share my poetry with boys
It made me feel special, like there was this
labryth to me
for them to hear me, my words, emotions, my
intelligence.
I felt like an enigma
I'm a complex breed, my arrogance coming full
circle through lined pages
small lips spoke such big, blabbered thoughts
they'd say good things, recognition for my soul.
Thats the only thing i had, worded puzzles of my
psyche
I am who I am.
I just don't read myself so thin anymore.

# Entity

A watered birth
a terencial triumph
I tryst to trust
but no bending to the warmth that set me to
rhythmic breaths
He is in the parallel
I equate and wait, right to left
He stops this hurt
I wish the breath that blows through his fire
sootes him from dismantling another
All of us are individually canvased
A muse for thier amusement
Harped strings
sonnets he played me
and left me unmended
No attuning yet.
I'm still in frequencies.

# Ribs

I have kept so many heartaches behind my
broken ribs
who do I share with, my other rib.
I'm left now to dust and remain, remains.
My consolation in consequence
actions I should've avoided
I took the bite,
left me with broken tongue
and now I barely speak.
I stay in the quiet realm of myself
it's safe but is it really.
I believe, I'm kidding myself into believing it
I'm almost there at times, then I remember
touch.
My embedded claws come out,
but I miss it all the same.

# April

Just saying nothing
doesn't excuse thoughtless occurrences
I could be vile then
unhealed anger is a weight worn into my
marrow
I had sunk effortlessly into your abusive nature
You, so obtuse an unsure of oneself
I'm not to blame
I was kerosene to your fire
like sulfur to flame
friction to your fiction
I'm still healing from you,
that's laughable in its own contentivness
I'll never be fully healed
I want to smother out your fire so badly
for the sake of others
I have a feeling you'll burn out eventually.
When it rains its pours,
Too bad it's not April yet.

# I'm on loan

I'm just a prism
through the cracks his evil seeped through
My feet still pressing upon the earth
I know that I am still
your dirt only sticks to my shoe
a cleanse
a watered Baptist
a steeple
a care
love
Most have a hard time understanding what they
cannot see
The unfathomable is a scary leave
fait turned mine to burden
My soul is mine still.
The many pieces stolen of myself were just on
loan
but I had no witnesses.

# Alma mater

This might not be long or poignant
or even to the point
I dont really have one
just writing
writing to make something happen
to fill a page
to use words
to fill a void
I already want to stop
halfway through
Thats my alma mater
halfway through
Never a closer
I cease to exist
I breathe, so I live
but I dont really live.
I didnt always feel this way
as of late
I told myself, self; you have to write at night
Use your euphinisms
sharpen that toolshed
create of what the creator gave you
To only try to use whimsical wise analogies is
exhausting
and I'm one line from the finish,
am I the tortoise or the hare.

# Nirvana

Some people have these honestly content
looking lives
how do they swing that
I guess thier lineage never pissed anyone off
I strive to make sense of why others have a
better offish start than others
how did they get so fortunate,
why others are starving in the streets
while they're popping bottles in their couture
their ensemble alone could feed and bed a
person for a week,
maybe even a month
depends on the labels,
we like our labels
druggie, no good, homeless loser.
They don't want to work
serves them right, right?
My sensitive nature
I notice all this too much,
it burdens my heart on a constant,
it eats me like sunday dinner.
They expect them to make a change off their
pocket change.
I want off this orbiting bullshit, this is for the
birds...

all I need is a bucket and a mop
That'll be nirvana
to clean this, shit up.

# Charlottes web

Justify the actions for the means
mean what you say
stick to it encased in a spiderweb
spindled like lost promises
That is exactly what I mean
this isn't charlotte's web
No help spelled out for you
Tangled webs trap the ones who deceive
always get them caught up.
They'll get stuck by the spider
Gotta love the symbolicnce,
Oh, irony is such a sticky bounce to never be
freed from.
Besides the fly on the wall.

# Extrovert

You know what I see
besides the Anima of oneself
I see, myself enveloped in it
I see the truth, times, lessons with drained out
egos
I see the world for what it is
not what I've been fixed to believe in
I can see right through a person without
conversation
I know their intentions just by the tone they
portray
I give way to their fixed mannerisms
The scariest part is knowing how they perceive
me
Thier perspective of my personality
Which I admit can be lowly and dry
I don't make enough serotonin to apply myself to
life
type A personality problems
If I wasn't aware, it wouldn't begrudge me so
badly,
but I am aware, and I spite myself in
conversation
which at all costs I try to avoid.
I miss connection so badly.

To only have been an extrovert...the life I
could've lived.

# Rose colored glasses

This will be a sign off piece
each day I awoke with a light smile,
now to awake
to a breathing overshadow
whose intellect is suppressive in a nature
that I cannot grow from
to be but once what I was,
guarded safely within lovely shades of
ignorance.
I hate sunglasses now,
and the smell of roses...disgust me.
My view obscured.